A DEATH IN GENEVA THAT PUT A NATION IN A COMA AND TRAUMATIZED AFRICA:

The Assassination of Félix-Roland Moumié and Cameroon's Unfinished Liberation

Janvier Tchouteu

TISI BOOKS

NEW YORK, RALEIGH, LONDON, AMSTERDAM

Non-Fiction Titles by Janvier T. Chando

ICONS AND VILLAINS: Recent Political Assassinations…
FALLEN HEROES: African Leaders Whose Assassinations…
UKRAINE: The Tug-of-War Between Russia and the West
Cameroon: France's Dysfunctional Puppet System in Africa
Cameroon: The Haunted Heart of Africa

Fiction Titles by Janvier Chando

The Usurper: and Other Stories
Triple Agent, Double Cross
Disciples of Fortune
The Union Moujik
Flash of the Sun
Fortune Calls
Fortune's Master
The Girl on the Trail
Fortune's Children
The Norilsk Bears
Me Before Them
The Grandmothers and Perfect Love
The Fire and Ice Legend
The Sweetest Madness
The Hunger Fire
The Shades of Fire
Father and Sons
Fateful Ties
The Verdict of Hades
His Majesty's Trial
Ngoko's Folly
The Usurper
The Dowry
I am Hated
The Oaf

Upcoming Titles by Janvier Chando

The Home Drifters
The Mortal Friends
The White Hawk
The Norilsk Bears

PUBLISHED BY TISI BOOKS
www.tisibooks.com

NEW YORK, RALEIGH, LONDON, AMSTERDAM

Printed in The United States of America

Acknowledgment

Special words of appreciation to Idris Mbebwo Doh with whom we discussed the Moumie legacy.

DEDICATION

The book is dedicated to all iconic and legendary leaders whose purposes were to serve humanity and advance the well-being of mankind, especially those who were cut short in their historic missions by the evil forces of this world.

A DEATH IN GENEVA THAT PUT A NATION IN A COMA AND TRAUMATIZED AFRICA:

The Assassination of Félix-Roland Moumié and Cameroon's Unfinished Liberation

Quotes

"If we fight to the death against an arbitrary integration of our country into the French colonial empire, it is because we want to remain the conquering defenders of the right of peoples to self-determination. We are thus, in the service of Kamerun and Africa...we are the true craftsmen of international detente. As revolutionary nationalists, we are fighting to realize for the Kamerun and for it alone, a true national "Independence" with "Unification" as a precondition, simultaneous or consecutive, but never excluded."

Ruben Um Nyobè

"We are not involved in this struggle only because we think that we will dismantle this system in the course of our life. We hope Cameroon changes tomorrow. But if it doesn't, we will be happy to know that we made the ground fertile for the next generation that will end the rot in this country, and then establish the 'NEW CAMEROON'."

Dr. Samuel F. Tchwenko, former UPCist and chief ideologue of the historic SDF of 1990-2002

"A people who are determined to fight for freedom and independence is invincible."
Ruben Um Nyobè

"Cameroon is not a country of slaves that no man can free."
Janvier Chouteu-Chando

"The enemy is not the one who is facing you with a sword in hand, that's the opponent. The enemy is the one behind you with a knife at your back."
Thomas Sankara

"...The world gets blessed every now and then with unique souls who though burdened by their invisible crosses, still have the extraordinary strength to forge ahead in life and give others a helping hand at the same time. Despite their tribulations, most of us think they are fine. Even when the weight of their crosses become unbearable, even when they proceed in a breathless manner, we still have a hard time understanding that they are drowning. In fact, we even condemn them for failing to sacrifice more..."
Janvier Chouteu-Chando, Disciples of Fortune

"Political independence has no meaning if it is not accompanied by rapid economic and social development."
Patrice Lumumba

"The worst thing that colonialism did was to cloud our view of our past."
Barack Obama

"Until the lions have their own historians, the history of the hunt will always glorify the hunter."

Chinua Achebe

"The characters in our other lives are ghosts that literature is reviving."

Olivier Weber

"Until the lions have their own historians, the history of the hunt will always glorify the hunter."

Chinua Achebe

"The characters in our other lives are ghosts that literature is reviving."

Olivier Weber

Contents

MAPS

Cameroon on a map of the world

Countries on the Map of Africa

Democracy in Africa

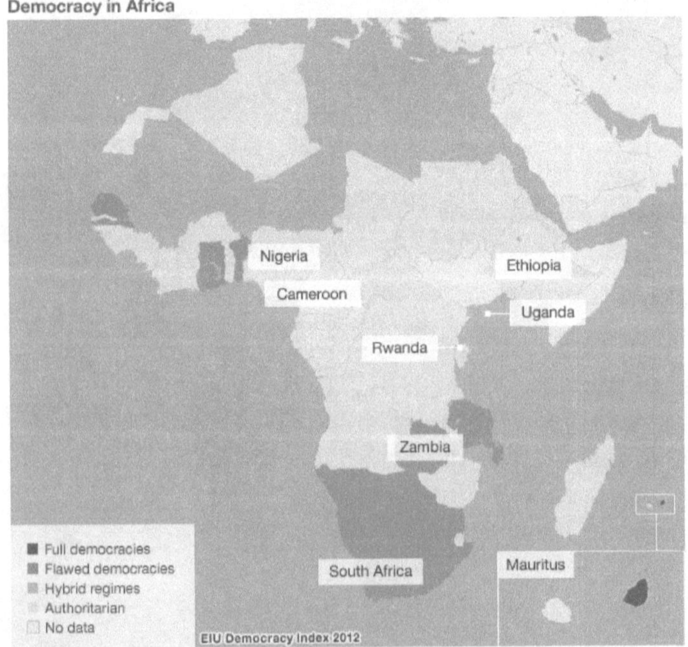

MAPS

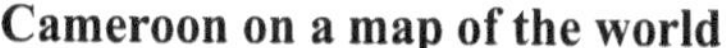

Cameroon on a map of the world

Countries on the Map of Africa

Democracy in Africa

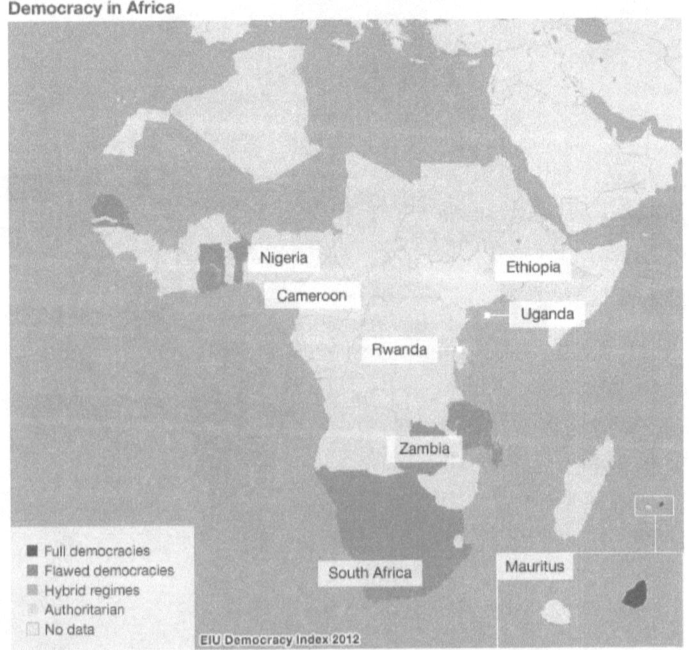

Cameroon over time

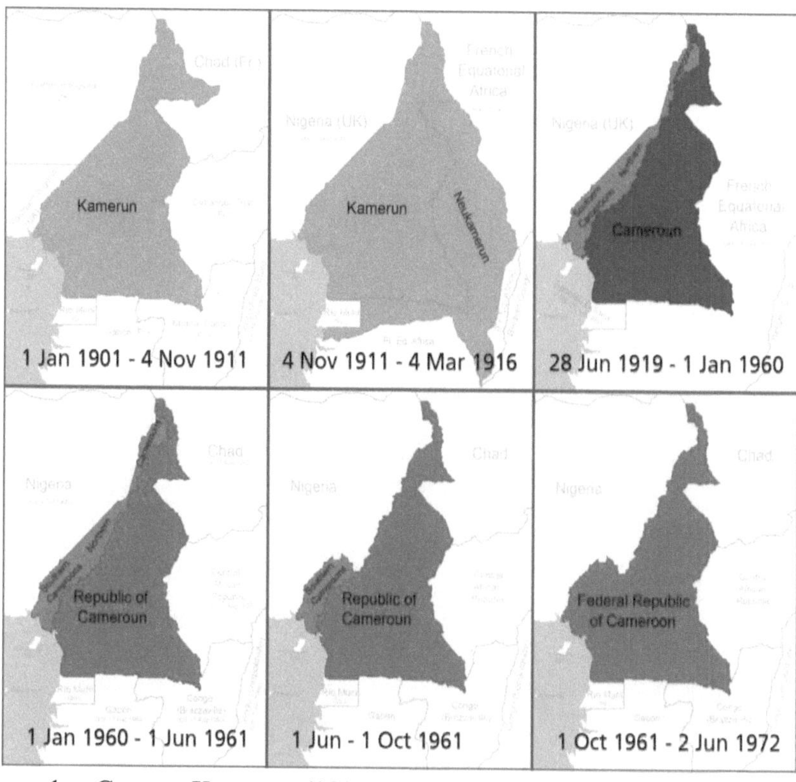

1. German Kamerun (1884-1911)
2. German Kamerun (1911-1916)
3. British Cameroons & French Cameroun: 1916-1960
4. British Cameroons & La Republique du Cameroun (1960-1961)
5. British Southern Cameroons & La Republique du Cameroun (1960-1961)
6. Reunited/Independent Cameroon today.

INTRODUCTION

In my search for the answer to why certain geopolitical flashpoints exist in the world, in my pry to know the reason(s) why some countries and the world in general experienced sudden and dramatic changes that led to war, instability or a reorientation of their domestic and foreign policies that not only affected these countries but also influence certain regions or the whole world, I explored political assassinations over the past dozens of decades that changed our world. By our world, I mean our communities, countries, regions, and humanity as a whole.

In treating the different assassinations that took place over the years, I used an approach characterized by political sociology, where I succinctly analyzed the historical and social factors that not only led to the assassinations, but that also arose from the killing of these historical figures. And from these factors, we are presented with an idea or pictures of how the society affected has evolved since the traumatic event(s).

From the backlashes that followed the assassination of historic, legendary, or iconic figures, we can learn something useful and come up with scenarios or what to expect as calamities if particular leaders are assassinated, and so act accordingly in preventing their assassinations.

Chapter One

Félix-Roland Moumié

Félix Moumié

UPC Leaders (L. to R.) front row: Castor Osendé Afana, Abel Kingué, Ruben Um Nyobé, Félix Moumié, and Ernest Ouandié

Born in 1926, Félix-Roland Moumié was an anti-colonialist Cameroonian leader and Pan-Africanist. His assassination in Geneva on November 03, 1960, by William Bechtel of the SDECE (the French Secret Service) with thallium is regarded as the most brazen crime committed by the French secret service abroad, and perhaps the biggest single blow suffered by Cameroonian civic-nationalists fighting for the liberation of the land from French neocolonial control.

Dr. Felix-Roland Moumié was the head of the UPC (*Union des Populations du Cameroun,* also called *Union du Peuple Camerounais* — "Union of the Populations of Cameroon") from 1958-1960. The UPC was the first historic political party to emerge from the territories of the former German colony of Kamerun. Founded in 1948, the UPC operated in both French Cameroun and British Cameroons — Trust Territories that emerged from the

1884-1916 former German Kamerun following its partition between Britain and France as agreed in the June 28, 1919 Treaty of Versailles, the most important of the peace treaties that brought World War I to a close, by formalizing the end of the state of war between Germany and the Allied Powers. The party's primary objective was the reunification and independence of British Cameroons and French Cameroun, Trust Territories that were the successors of the League of Nations mandates, and that came into being when the League of Nations ceased to exist in 1946.

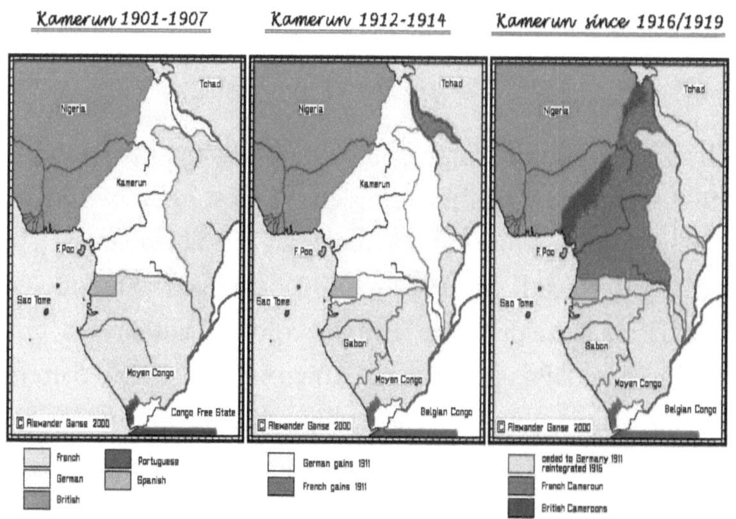

Chapter Two

The French Trusteeship administration banned the UPC in 1955, accusing it of fomenting civil unrest, thereby forcing the party into exile in the summer of 1955. However, The UPC resurfaced in 1956 and challenged France via international media. The British colonial authorities also banned the UPC in British Cameroons in 1958, thereby forcing most of its leadership that escaped French Cameroun and sought sanctuary in British Cameroons, to flee to Egypt, Ghana, China, and other countries that were supportive of the Cameroonian cause for its reunification and independence.

Ruben Um Nyobé, the party's leader and Secretary-General; Ernest Ouandié and Abel Kingué, the party's two vice presidents; and Felix Moumié pledged to carry on with the struggle for the reunification and independence of French Cameroun and British Cameroons, despite France's resolve to divide and rule the peoples of the former German Kamerun. After all, the UPC commanded the support of most of the people of French Cameroun, and its offshoots and sister parties in British Cameroons commanded the support of the electorate there. In fact, more than 80% of educated Cameroonians supported the party and its cause for the reunification and independence of the lands of the former German Kamerun.

However, the party received its first major trauma when three years after the ban, at a time that some pundits were beginning to think that France would allow the party to start operating again as a legal political entity, the security forces of the French Trusteeship administration assassinated the UPC's first historic leader Ruben Um Nyobé on September 13, 1958, near his home village of Boumnyebel in the Bassaland.

Chapter Three

So, when Dr. Felix-Roland Moumié succeeded Ruben Um Nyobé, he was forced to operate from exile, even though the UPC was the only party in French Cameroun that enjoyed the overwhelming support of French Camerounians, and even though it was also the only political party in that part of the former German Kamerun that shared a similar program with sister parties or offshoots in British Cameroons. Undeterred, he challenged France's crackdown on the UPC in a more determined manner, so that UPC partisans were in control of much of the countryside of the southern half of French Cameroun before France handed French Cameroun's political control or sovereignty to its puppet Ahmadou Ahidjo, declared the land independent on January 01, 1960, and at the same time concluded a series of socio-economic, political, and military agreements with the infant state that virtually made it a backyard of France.

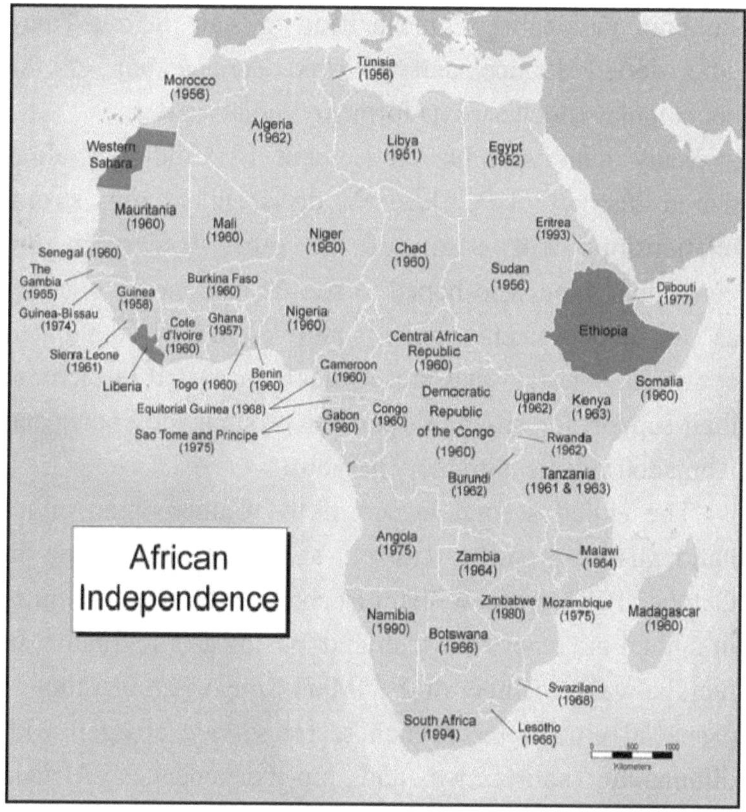

Considered by some as the "African Che Guevara in the making", Félix Moumié was an astute leader as well as a great organizer who before his death, had met that summer of 1960 with Ernesto Che Guevara, the Argentine international revolutionary and second-in-command in the new anti-American and anti-Western government of Fidel Castro's Cuba. In addition to that development, the

Cameroonian partisan leader had successfully developed a special rapport with the bellicose Egyptian president Gamal Abdel Nasser, the Pan-Africanist president of Ghana Kwame Nkrumah, the unwavering Patrice Lumumba of Congo-Kinshasa (the former Belgian Congo), and the stubborn nationalist Guinean head of state Sékou Touré who defied France and whisked Guinea out of the neocolonial clutches of its former colonial master.

Many pundits think France and its Cold-War allies feared the new UPC leader's drive, in forging strong relationships with some of the other leaders in the communist bloc who hoped to see Africa emerge one day as an economically united and politically integrated continent. The fact that those leaders promised to increase their support for Moumié's partisan group made France and Ahmadou Ahidjo extremely nervous.

The exiled second leader of the Cameroonian civic-nationalist movement was on a mission to Europe in October 1960, when William Bechtel invited him to dinner in a hotel in Geneva, Switzerland, posing as a journalist. In fact, he was a member of the "Main Rouge," an offshoot of a special unit in the French secret service charged with eliminating anti-French and pro-independence African nationalists and their supporters in Europe.

Distracted by a summon to the phone by a restaurant staff, Moumié left his unfinished drink that Bechtel contaminated by pouring a lethal dose of thallium into it. But Moumié did not drink it upon his return. So, Bechtel created another distraction, during which he poured another dose of thallium into Moumié's wine. Moumié ended up gulping down both drinks and died in a Geneva hospital on November 3, 1960, days before his return to Guinea, and much earlier than his killers had planned. The fact that the Cameroonian liberation leader took an overdose of the poison thwarted the plot France had hatched to blame Felix Moumié's death on Guinean president Sekou Touré, who had been acting as the UPC leader's host during his exile in the Guinean capital of Conakry.

Félix Moumié's body is flown to Guinea for burial

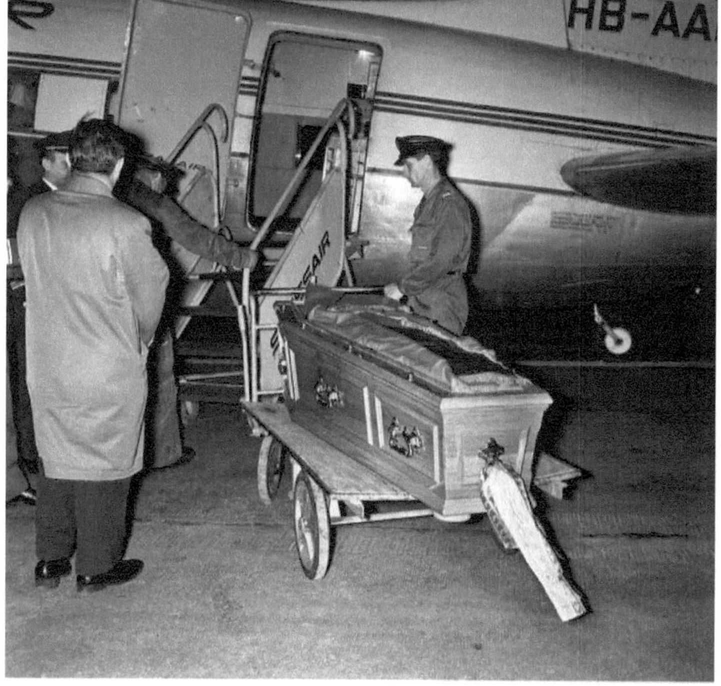

Chapter Four

Félix Moumié's assassination would be followed three months later by the horrendous assassination of Patrice Lumumba of the former Belgian Congo. The deaths of these two African civic-nationalists with a Pan-Africanist vision would be followed by a bloody repression of the popular resistance to the neo-colonial regimes in their respective countries.

With the execution of Félix Moumié's successor Ernest Ouandie in January 1971, the neo-colonial counter-offensive against the anti-colonialist movements in the heart of Africa would be over, spelling victory for the neocolonial forces. This new reality would have disastrous consequences not only in the Central African region but throughout Africa. Francophone Sub-Saharan Africa has not dared to oppose French neocolonialism since the defeat of Cameroonian civic-nationalism and France's imposition of a mafia-like system of control over its former colonies that makes use of French puppets who are not accountable to their people.

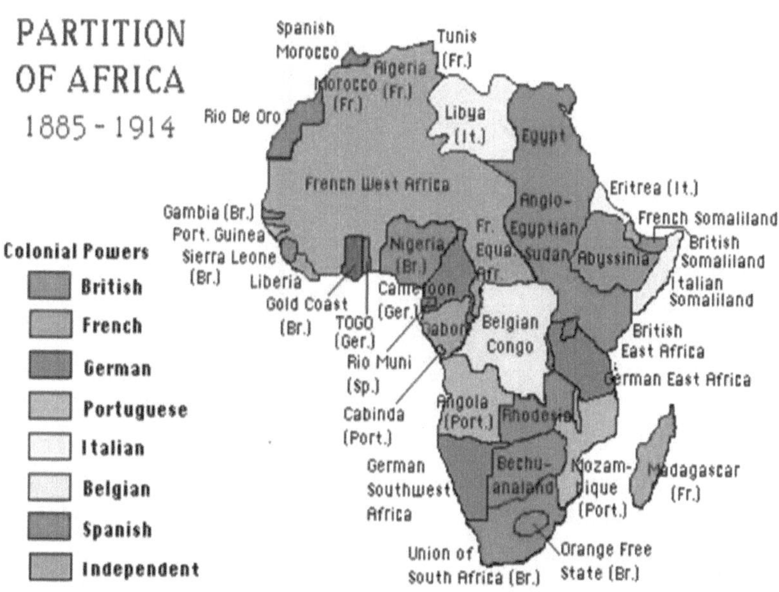

The death of Félix Moumié, the retention of the French ban on the UPC, the UPC's 1958 expulsion from British Cameroons, and the return to power in France of the French legend and neocolonialist General Charles De Gaulle made the realization of the Kamerunian dream of reunification, independence and development seem impossible. However, offshoots of the UPC in British Cameroons and the

Cameroonian civic-nationalists in British Southern Cameroons realized the reunification dream by championing the campaign in the United Nations-sponsored plebiscite or referendum for the vote to reunite British Southern Cameroons with the one-year-old Republic of Cameroun, the former French Cameroun that got its independence on January 01, 1960, under the anti-UPC government of the French puppet Ahmadou Ahidjo.

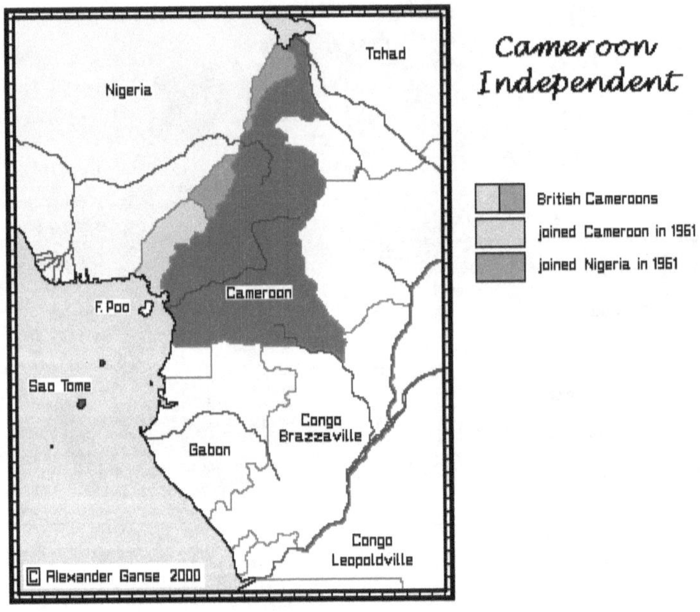

11-12 February 1961 British Cameroons Plebiscite
Main Points: Voters were asked if they wanted to unite with Nigeria or Cameroon when independence is granted to the two regions.

Northern Cameroons
Registered Voters   292,985
Total Votes (Voter   Not Available (N/A)
Turnout)
Invalid/Blank Votes   Not Available
Total Valid Votes   243,955

<u>Southern Cameroons</u>

Registered Voters	349,652
Total Votes (Voter Turnout)	Not Available (N/A)
Invalid/Blank Votes	Not Available
Total Valid Votes	331,312

Results	Northern Cameroons		Southern Cameroons	
	Number of Votes	% of Votes	Number of Votes	% of Votes
Union with the Federation of Nigeria	146,296	59.97%	97,741	29.50%
Union with the Republic of Cameroon	97,659	40.03%	233,571	70.50%

In fact, even though inferiorly armed, the UPC led an effective guerilla campaign that had at the end of 1959, confined complete French control in the south of the country only to the cities and towns, leaving the villages and countryside under the control of the UPC. And since the UN Trusteeship Agreement set a cap on the number of troops the French Army could have in the territory, France decided to precipitate the granting of independence to French Cameroon. However, it granted French Cameroun independence on January 01, 1960, under its puppet Ahmadou Ahidjo, and at the same time compelled Ahidjo to sign a secretive pact with France, an agreement with economic, political, and military components that among other things, allowed France to multiply the number of French troops it had stationed in former French Cameroun, called the Republic of Cameroon thereafter. The French army would reinforce its presence in the land by increasing the number of its soldiers and hardware there, and by speeding up the recruitment and training of a French-led local Cameroonian Army. These Franco-Cameroonian armies would defeat the insurgents in its major strongholds in the Bassaland in 1960 and the Bamilekeland from 1962-1964, by inflicting heavy losses on the UPC and the civilian populations through their indiscriminate bombing of both the guerilla camps and the civil communities, a scorched-earth policy per se that some historians and various pundits consider a French-led genocide against certain forces and populations of areas of Cameroon that opposed France's neocolonialist plans for Cameroon.

The UPC realized by 1965 that it could no longer win the armed conflict against the French Army and the Cameroonian Army France created for the puppet Ahmadou Ahidjo regime. Prevaricated efforts at achieving peace through peace talks would lure Felix Moumié's successor Ernest Ouandie out of the bush, leading to his surrender/capture, and then execution in January 1971, thereby ending the UPC armed struggle against France for the reunification, independence and freedom of the territories of the former German Kamerun, a conflict that resulted in the deaths of more than half a million Cameroonian lives in what some pundits view as "Cameroon's Unfinished Liberation", since those and the heirs of those who campaigned and fought for Cameroon's reunification and independence have been prevented from power in the country ever since.

Chapter Five

Cameroonians from the English-speaking part of reunited Cameroon soon realized that they had been deceived and subjugated by France and her puppet, like the defeated and subdued populations of the French-speaking part of the country, and that they too were now under the suffocating yoke of a French-imposed system managed by the dictatorship of France's puppet Ahmadou Ahidjo. Paul Biya, another French marionette, and Ahmadou Ahidjo's successor from the orders of France has been in power since 1982 and has exacerbated the suffocation of Cameroon even further. Close to sixty years after, Cameroon is still under the control of the anti-UPC forces put in place by France — these are Cameroonians who played no role, whether as moderates or as radicals, in the nationalist struggle for the land's reunification and independence. In fact, France aided its puppets in establishing a police state to impose their rule, which explains why Cameroon has never experienced rule under a head of state that is or was the choice of the people.

The mafia continues. The country that embodies Africa's daring spirit is still in the grips of the forces that were against its quest for liberation, development, and partnership with other progressive forces of the world.

The assassinations of Ruben Um Nyobé, Félix Moumié, Patrice Lumumba, Castor Osendé Afana, Ernest Ouandie, and tens of thousands of Congolese and Cameroonian civic-nationalists was after all a successful campaign by neocolonial powers to destroy Africa's genuine independent development, as defeating the anti-colonial movements in these countries weakened the pan-Africanist drive to create an African economic union and to integrate the continent politically. Despite any indications or expectations to the contrary, the Cameroon of Nyobè/Moumié/Ouandie that was never realized, and the Congo of Lumumba that failed to be, would have been at the geographic, economic, and political center of the African Union that is still the vision of many progressive Africans who hope to see the continent secure a place of respect for itself in the growing multi-polar world.

Today, Félix Moumié's sarcophagus is still missing in what was his resting place in the cemetery in Conakry, Guinea. Albert Kingue is still buried in Cairo, Egypt. Ruben Um Nyobé, Ernest Ouandie, Castor Osendé Afana, and the other leaders of the UPC killed by the Franco-Ahidjo forces are hardly acknowledged, let alone recognized in the annals of Cameroonian history, even though their names grace streets and infrastructures in other countries of Africa and the world.

Six decades after, Cameroonians rising up to challenge the

mafia state still see Felix-Roland Moumié and the other historic Union-Nationalist leaders that got killed, exiled, or undermined by France and the puppets it imposed on the country, as the forces to emulate in their drive to dismantle the system imposed on the people. Paul Biya leads the system and its authoritarian political establishment today, a puppet imposed by France on the people of Cameroon. The second Cameroonian president has been in power for forty-seven years (thirty-seven years as the president or head of state since 1982, and ten years as prime minister of the only country in Africa where its head of state has never been the choice of the people, but rather an imposition by neocolonialists).

Democracy Index: Africa and the World

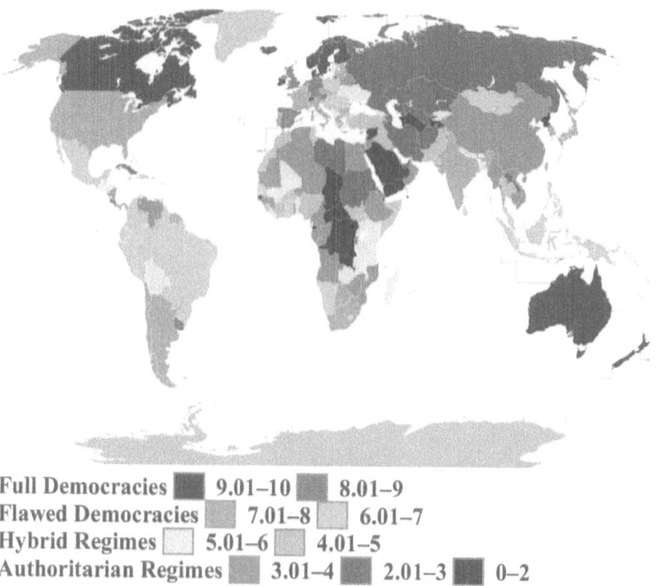

African Countries

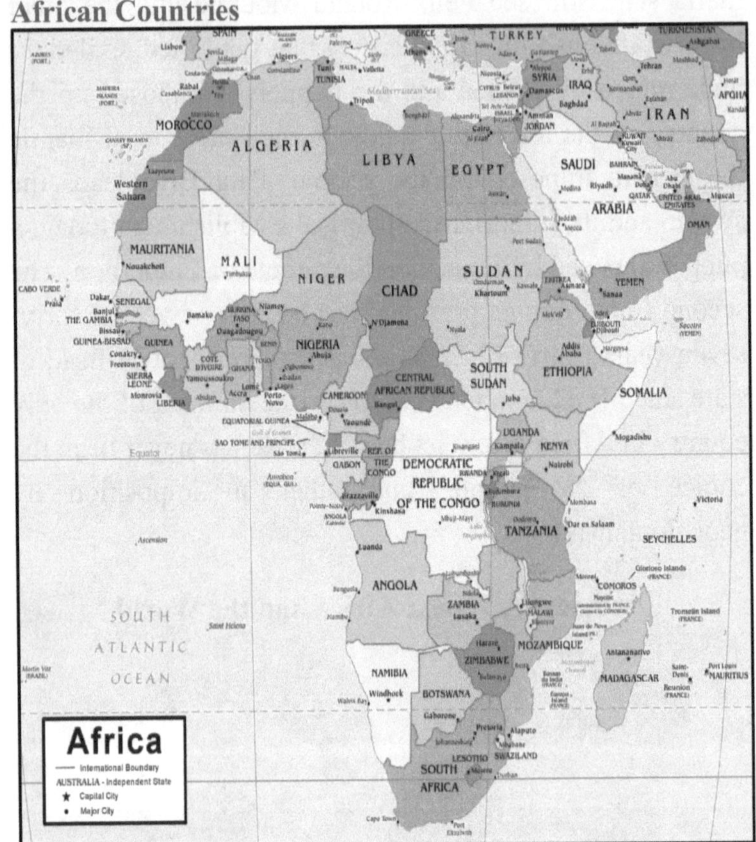